IT'S MY STATE!

VIRGINIA

David C. King

Stephanie Fitzgerald

Marshall Cavendish
Benchmark
New York

Copyright © 2011 Marshall Cavendish Corporation

Published by Marshall Cavendish Benchmark
An imprint of Marshall Cavendish Corporation

Website: www.marshallcavendish.us

This publication represents the opinions and views of the authors based on their personal experience, knowledge, and research. The information in this book serves as a general guide only. The authors and publisher have used their best efforts in preparing this book and disclaim liability rising directly and indirectly from the use and application of this book.

Other Marshall Cavendish Offices:
Marshall Cavendish International (Asia) Private Limited, 1 New Industrial Road, Singapore 536196 • Marshall Cavendish International (Thailand) Co Ltd. 253 Asoke, 12th Flr, Sukhumvit 21 Road, Klongtoey Nua, Wattana, Bangkok 10110, Thailand • Marshall Cavendish (Malaysia) Sdn Bhd, Times Subang, Lot 46, Subang Hi-Tech Industrial Park, Batu Tiga, 40000 Shah Alam, Selangor Darul Ehsan, Malaysia

Marshall Cavendish is a trademark of Times Publishing Limited

All websites were available and accurate when this book was sent to press.

Library of Congress Cataloging-in-Publication Data
King, David C.
      Virginia / David C. King and Stephanie Fitzgerald. — 2nd ed.
         p. cm. — (It's my state!)
      Includes index.
      ISBN 978-1-60870-060-8
        1. Virginia—Juvenile literature. I. Fitzgerald, Stephanie. II. Title.
   F226.3.K56 2011
   975.5—dc22   2010003933

Second Edition developed for Marshall Cavendish Benchmark by RJF Publishing LLC (www.RJFpublishing.com)
Series Designer, Second Edition: Tammy West/Westgraphix LLC
Editor, Second Edition: Emily Dolbear

All maps, illustrations, and graphics © Marshall Cavendish Corporation. Maps and artwork on pages 6, 34, 35, 76, 77, and back cover by Christopher Santoro. Map and graphics on pages 9 and 47 by Westgraphix LLC.

The photographs in this book are used by permission and through the courtesy of:
Front cover: S. Borisov and Terrie L. Zeller (inset)/Shutterstock.
Alamy: David Robert Eastley, 15; Pat & Chuck Blackley, 21, 49, 54; M. Timothy O'Keefe, 24; Blend Images, 44, 53; Jeff Greenberg, 46, 47, 64; Frank Tozier, 52; Chris A Crumley, 55; Jim West, 66. **Corbis:** Leonard de Selva, 37. **Getty Images:** Richard Ellis, 4; Joe Drivas, 5 (top); Tom Schierlitz, 5 (bottom); Cameron Davidson, 8; MPI/Stringer/Hulton Archive, 10, 39; Don Klumpp, 11; Karen Bleier/AFP, 13; Altrendo Nature, 17; Jeremy Woodhouse, 18; Medford Taylor/National Geographic, 19; Sue Flood, 22 (top); Kate Mathis, 22 (bottom); Nick Caloyianis/National Geographic, 23; Theodore de Bry/The Bridgeman Art Library, 26; SuperStock, 27, 33; Time & Life Pictures, 31; Hulton Archive, 40; New York Times Co./Hulton Archive, 41; Erik Simonsen, 42; Stock Montage/Hulton Archive, 50; Manny Millan/Sports Illustrated, 51 (top); Jim Watson/AFP, 51 (bottom); Joseph Sohm-Visions of America, 59; Michael Kleih Photography, 61; Baerbel Schmidt, 62; Yellow Dog Productions, 65; Peter Essick, 67; G Richardson/Robert Harding, 69; Panoramic Images, 70-1; Nicholas Eveleigh, 72; Danita Delimont, 73 (top); Matt Bowman, 73 (bottom); Anne Rippy, 74-5. **Shutterstock:** Dave Newman, 56.

Printed in Malaysia (T).
135642

CONTENTS

State Tree and Flower: American Dogwood

Also called the flowering dogwood, this tree is best known for its beautiful blossoms. The flowers, white or pink with small yellow centers, are a sure sign of spring. Dogwoods grow throughout Virginia in the wild as well as in neighborhood gardens and yards.

State Bird: Northern Cardinal

Common throughout the eastern states, this bright red songbird is known for the pointed crest on its head and for its deep red feathers. Females, which are less brilliantly colored than males, are usually dull reddish brown. This cardinal's song is a clear, piercing whistle.

State Dog: American Foxhound

This hunting dog can trace its roots to colonial times. The English brought hounds with them to America in the 1600s. More than one hundred years later, the descendants of those dogs were bred with French hounds that had been given to George Washington. The resulting breed, the American foxhound, is a scent dog that still takes part in fox hunts in Virginia.

State Shell: Virginia Oyster

The Virginia oyster was a crucial food source for the American Indians who first inhabited the area. Today, it is one of the most valuable shellfish for North American fishers. Whether eaten raw, cooked, smoked, on the shell, or from a can, oysters are a favorite food along the Atlantic Coast.

State Insect: Tiger Swallowtail Butterfly

The beautiful tiger swallowtail is one of the most common butterflies in the eastern United States. The bright yellow and black stripes on its body and wings make the tiger swallowtail easy to identify. The largest species (a southern subspecies) can have a wingspan of more than 6 inches (15 centimeters).

State Beverage: Milk

In 1982, milk became Virginia's official beverage. Almost 100,000 dairy cows are located on farms across the state—the greatest numbers are in Rockingham County. These cows produce almost 2 billion pounds (900 million kilograms) of milk in a single year.

The Old Dominion

Virginia has 39,594 square miles (102,548 square kilometers) of land area. It is the thirty-seventh largest state in land area. It is made up of ninety-five counties, plus thirty-nine independent cities. Richmond is the state capital, but Virginia Beach is the city with the biggest population.

The state includes a remarkable variety of landforms for its size. The coastal region includes marshy lowlands, beautiful sand beaches, and a large swamp area. Moving inland, the lowlands change into the rolling hills of the Piedmont. Still farther west are two mountain ranges with dramatic views and hundreds of miles of hiking trails. Nestled between the Blue Ridge Mountains and the Allegheny Mountains is the scenic and fertile Shenandoah Valley, one of America's great natural treasures.

Virginia's Eastern Shore

The geography of eastern Virginia is dominated by Chesapeake Bay—a huge arm of the Atlantic Ocean. The bay reaches more than 200 miles (320 km) into the North American continent. The long, narrow strip of land that forms the eastern boundary of the bay is called

Quick Facts

VIRGINIA BORDERS

North	Maryland
	West Virginia
	Washington, D.C.
South	North Carolina
	Tennessee
East	Maryland
	Atlantic Ocean
West	Kentucky
	West Virginia

The Chesapeake Bay Bridge-Tunnel, opened to traffic in 1964, runs more than 17 miles (27 km).

the Delmarva Peninsula. The word *Delmarva* was created out of the names of the three states that occupy the strip of land—Delaware, Maryland, and Virginia. Some Virginians call the region the Eastern Shore. Until bridges were built connecting the Eastern Shore to the mainland in 1964, residents there and on the nearby islands were quite isolated.

Offshore, or barrier, islands give this sliver of land some protection from Atlantic storms. They include Assateague and Chincoteague islands, which are famous for their semiwild Chincoteague ponies.

Chesapeake Bay

Chesapeake Bay is a unique body of water. It is America's largest estuary—a partially enclosed area where fresh river waters and salty ocean waters meet. More than 150 of Virginia's major rivers and streams empty into the Chesapeake, including the Potomac, Rappahannock, York, and James rivers.

The warm, shallow waters of the bay are filled with schools of fish and large colonies of shellfish—oysters, clams, and the famous Chesapeake blue crabs. On

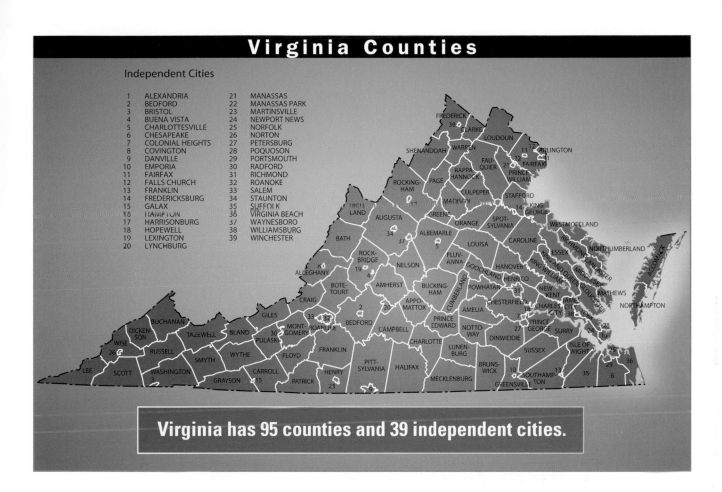

Virginia Counties

Independent Cities

#	City	#	City
1	ALEXANDRIA	21	MANASSAS
2	BEDFORD	22	MANASSAS PARK
3	BRISTOL	23	MARTINSVILLE
4	BUENA VISTA	24	NEWPORT NEWS
5	CHARLOTTESVILLE	25	NORFOLK
6	CHESAPEAKE	26	NORTON
7	COLONIAL HEIGHTS	27	PETERSBURG
8	COVINGTON	28	POQUOSON
9	DANVILLE	29	PORTSMOUTH
10	EMPORIA	30	RADFORD
11	FAIRFAX	31	RICHMOND
12	FALLS CHURCH	32	ROANOKE
13	FRANKLIN	33	SALEM
14	FREDERICKSBURG	34	STAUNTON
15	GALAX	35	SUFFOLK
16	HAMPTON	36	VIRGINIA BEACH
17	HARRISONBURG	37	WAYNESBORO
18	HOPEWELL	38	WILLIAMSBURG
19	LEXINGTON	39	WINCHESTER
20	LYNCHBURG		

Virginia has 95 counties and 39 independent cities.

most days of the year, this inland sea swarms with sailboats, speedboats, and fishing vessels.

A broad inlet connects Chesapeake Bay with the James River to form Hampton Roads, one of the world's largest natural harbors. In 1862, during the Civil War, Hampton Roads was the scene of the world's first clash between two ironclad warships. The USS *Monitor* faced off against the CSS *Virginia* (often called the *Merrimack*—its name while part of the U.S. fleet) in an effort to protect the USS *Minnesota*. Neither side won the battle, but the *Minnesota* remained

Quick Facts

THE MIGHTY JAMES
The James River stretches 340 miles (547 km) through Virginia. It is one of the longest rivers in America that begins and ends in the same state.

Union troops watch the battle between their naval vessel the *Monitor* and the Confederate ironclad *Virginia*.

unharmed. Both the *Monitor* and the *Virginia* survived the battle without much damage—and ushered in a new era of shipbuilding.

The Tidewater Region

A belt of lowland called the Coastal Plain, which stretches from New York to Florida, characterizes the Atlantic Coast. Virginians call their portion of the Coastal Plain the Tidewater because ocean tides reach all the way into Chesapeake Bay and Virginia's four main rivers. From north to south, Virginia's coast measures about 112 miles (180 km), but all the inlets and bays, plus the Eastern Shore, create a coastline of more than 3,000 miles (almost 5,000 km).

The state's largest urban area is on the southern part of the Tidewater, including the port cities of Newport News and Norfolk, as well as Virginia Beach.

Virginia Beach has about 35 miles (56 km) of beautiful white sand beach lined with modern high-rise apartment buildings. Huge ports are located in Newport News and Norfolk, which is also home to the world's largest naval station.

South of the James River is an enormous wetland named the Great Dismal Swamp. This protected area is nearly 600 square miles (1,500 sq km) and extends into North Carolina. In 1763, George Washington surveyed the swamp and saw its potential for timber production. He formed a company called the Dismal Swamp Land Company to drain and log parts of the swamp. Logging proved very successful and, along with commercial and residential development, destroyed much of the ecosystem. The remaining area, which became the Great Dismal Swamp National Wildlife Refuge in 1974, is less than half the size of the original swamp.

From the mid–1600s through the 1800s, sprawling farms called plantations were built on the banks of the Tidewater rivers. Tobacco was the major cash crop of the early plantations, and after 1800, wheat became important.

This huge battleship is docked near the National Maritime Center in Norfolk, the location of the world's largest naval station.

These plantations, some of which still exist, were like independent villages. Each had its own orchard, vegetable garden, blacksmith shop, and carpenter—as well as a church. Rivers such as the James, York, and Rappahannock served as highways. Sailing ships carried the planters' crops to market towns and brought back merchandise from other East Coast cities and from Europe. Boats navigated the rivers to the Fall Line—the point where the soft Coastal Plain meets the harder rock of the inland hill country.

The Piedmont

West of the Tidewater is a region called the Piedmont. It covers the central third of the state. The Piedmont features a rolling landscape that is about 50 miles (80 km) wide in the north, broadening to about 100 miles (160 km) wide in the south. The Piedmont stretches from the Blue Ridge Mountains in the west to the Fall Line.

As the Tidewater region filled with settlers in the early 1700s, pioneer families moved into the Piedmont. Most started small farms, but there were also a number of tobacco plantations. Family-owned farms, including apple and peach orchards, still cover the foothills of the Blue Ridge Mountains today. Some of the Piedmont is also now known as "horse country," famous for its traditions of foxhunting and horse breeding.

The Western Mountains

The Blue Ridge Mountains extend from Harper's Ferry, West Virginia, south into Georgia. The mountains form one of America's outstanding scenic areas. Two of the nation's most scenic roads wind along the crest of these mountains and upland meadows. The northern road, Skyline Drive, twists and turns for 105 miles (169 km), with a maximum speed limit of 35 miles per hour (56 kph). The southern road, the Blue Ridge Parkway, extends another 469 miles (755 km), from Shenandoah National Park in northern Virginia to Great Smoky Mountains National Park in North Carolina. In general, the Blue Ridge Mountains vary in height from 2,000 to 4,000 feet (600 to 1,200 meters). One exceptionally high point in the range—and the highest point in the state—is Mount Rogers, which is 5,729 feet (1,746 m) above sea level.

The Blue Ridge Mountains and the more rugged Allegheny Mountains to the west are among the oldest mountains in the world. Over thousands of years, the forces of wind and water slowly wore away the jagged peaks to create more gentle landforms. The two scenic roads through the Blue

A tourist reads an information board along Skyline Drive overlooking the Blue Ridge Mountains.

Ridge provide breathtaking views of the Piedmont hills to the east and the Alleghenies to the west. The leaves of the hardwood trees on the slopes of the Blue Ridge—maple, hickory, white oak, and others—turn dazzling colors in the autumn.

The Allegheny Mountains, one of the ranges in the Appalachian chain, are on Virginia's border with Kentucky. For America's pioneers, these mountains formed a more imposing barrier than the Blue Ridge. It was not until 1775 that Daniel Boone led a group of woodsmen to blaze—or create—a trail through a pass called the Cumberland Gap from southwest Virginia into what became Kentucky. Thousands of families followed Boone's so-called Wilderness Road.

The Shenandoah Valley

When the first pioneers entered the Shenandoah Valley around 1700, they saw herds of bison roaming fertile grasslands watered by the Shenandoah River. By the late 1700s, the bison—and most American Indian groups—had retreated farther west. Land-hungry settlers poured into the valley and established small family-owned farms, many of which are still in operation today.

The northern end of the valley, which is approximately 150 miles (240 km) long, is anchored by Winchester, the capital of Virginia's well-known apple-orchard region. The orchards and wheat fields of the Shenandoah were important to the South during the Civil War. The valley also formed a natural north-south highway for the South's armies.

In June 1863, for example, the famous Confederate general Robert E. Lee led his Army of Northern Virginia north through the valley, using the Blue Ridge Mountains to shield his movements from the North's armies in the east. The next month, after the Confederate defeat at Gettysburg, Pennsylvania, Lee used the valley for his retreat.

Today, the Shenandoah Valley is a popular tourist area. The valley is dotted with Civil War battle sites and historic homes, including the

Quick Facts

LIFESAVING BRIDGE

According to legend, it was Monacan Indians who first discovered the Natural Bridge. During a clash with other Indian tribes, the Monacans reached Cedar Creek with nowhere to go and prayed to the Great Spirit for protection. The bridge suddenly appeared, allowing the women and children to cross the ravine while the Monacan warriors stood to fight. After defeating their enemies, the warriors followed the women and children across the bridge.

In 1998, the U.S. Department of the Interior designated Virginia's Natural Bridge a National Historic Landmark.

birthplace of President Woodrow Wilson and the headquarters of Civil War general Thomas "Stonewall" Jackson.

Visitors are also drawn to natural wonders such as the Natural Bridge, a limestone arch located 215 feet (66 m) above Cedar Creek. Before he became president of the United States, Thomas Jefferson was so fascinated by the Natural Bridge that he purchased it from the British government in 1774. He called it "the most sublime of nature's works." The region also has popular limestone caves, including Luray Caverns, where musicians play the Great Stalacpipe Organ, a musical instrument made from stalactites (structures made by minerals and water over the years).

Climate

The Virginia climate offers something for everyone. Along the coast, people enjoy long summers and mild winters. Farmers like the Tidewater growing season, which lasts up to eight months—three months longer than in the western part of the state. Although the Tidewater receives only a few inches of snow every year, the mountains see up to 23 inches (58 cm).

The overall climate of Virginia is mild. But the ocean affects weather and climate, making summers generally cooler near the coast than farther inland. The ocean also makes coastal winters less severe. In the mountain regions, the higher the altitude, the lower the temperature is likely to be. January temperatures on the Eastern Shore, for example, close to sea level, average about 42 degrees Fahrenheit (6 degrees Celsius), while in the mountains, the average January temperature is about 31 °F (–1 °C).

Virginia Wildlife

Forests cover about 65 percent of Virginia's land area (most of which is considered "unusable" land). Some of the state's most common trees there include oaks, pines, maples, hickory, and beech. In the fall, the leaves on many of these trees turn brilliant shades of orange, red, or yellow. The state has many different types of plants, including ferns and native grasses. In warmer

Luray Caverns have many cave formations. Stalactites look like icicles hanging from a ceiling, and stalagmites rise from a cave floor. Sometimes the two grow together and form columns.

The Blue Ridge Parkway, which winds its way hundreds of miles, is most colorful in autumn.

months, when flowering plants are blooming, wisteria, lilies, azaleas, mountain laurels, and bluebells make colorful additions to the state's impressive scenery.

Thanks to its varied landscapes and ecosystems, Virginia is home to an incredible array of wildlife. Animals such as deer and raccoons can be found in most areas—including the suburbs. The state's fourteen wildlife refuges include all types of habitats from forests to marshes. Black bears, river otters, bobcats, and many bird species live in remote places such as the Great Dismal Swamp. Virginia Beach is a great place to see pods of dolphins frolicking in the surf. The area also has wonderful bird-watching.

Chesapeake Bay is on the Atlantic flyway, the path that many birds take when traveling south to warmer temperatures for the winter and then traveling north again in spring. In spring and autumn, thousands of migrating birds pause to rest on the area's many islands and on the Eastern Shore. More than two hundred species have been identified, including many kinds of shorebirds. Geese, ducks, and other water birds make their homes in or near Virginia waterways.

The state's bodies of water are home to fish and amphibians. Trout, pike, perch, sunfish, bass, and catfish live in the lakes, rivers, ponds, and streams. Striped bass, American shad, and herring swim through the waters of Chesapeake Bay. Moist land in swamps and near lakes, rivers, and streams is ideal for amphibians such as frogs, salamanders, and newts.

Great egrets wade through the marshes of Assateague Island.

The People's Park

Many Virginians are concerned about the state's plants and animals. In the 1920s, outsiders who had hiked, camped, hunted, and fished in the Blue Ridge began urging the state and federal governments to turn the region into a park. In 1926, the U.S. Congress authorized the creation of a national park but only if the land was donated. Hundreds of Virginians went to work, urging people to buy 1 acre (0.4 hectare) of Blue Ridge land for six dollars and then donate it to the government. The state government also gained land for the park by buying farms from those who wanted to leave.

Construction on the park began in 1931 when Herbert Hoover, who had a fishing camp in the area, was president of the United States. When President Franklin D. Roosevelt took office in 1933, he also eagerly promoted the park. A government-run program sent hundreds of young unemployed men into the Blue Ridge to create camping areas and hiking trails. The government also paid to relocate more than 450 families who lived in the area. But the government also allowed older residents to remain on their land for the rest of their lives. (The last elderly mountain resident died in 1979.)

President Roosevelt dedicated Shenandoah National Park on July 3, 1936. The park is a sanctuary for one hundred varieties of trees and more than one thousand flowering plants. In fact, park personnel say that the Shenandoah has more species of plants than all of Europe. There are 500 miles (800 km) of trails for hiking and horseback riding and dozens of trout streams.

Herbert Hoover's dream of a road through the region has become the Skyline Drive and Blue Ridge Parkway. Whether they are driving along these roads or hiking through the park, Virginians and visitors can get a superb view of the state's natural beauty.

Hikers in Shenandoah National Park take a break.

Plants & Animals

Black Bear

Shenandoah National Park has one of the densest black bear populations in the United States. (Density refers to the number of bears per square mile.) Black bears live throughout the state of Virginia. In fact, they are so common that the state allows annual black bear hunting to help control the population.

Lady's Slipper

This delicate plant, with its bright, boot-shaped flowers, grows well in Virginia's moist soil. Lady's slippers come in many different colors and go by many different names, including American valerian and moccasin flower. American Indians and early settlers used the plant as a drug to make them feel calmer and sleep better.

American Chestnut

The American chestnut tree was once the most abundant tree in the hardwood forests of eastern North America. People ate chestnuts and fed them to their livestock. They also harvested the nuts as a cash crop and cut the trees for lumber. Disaster struck in 1904 when a chestnut disease killed off all the trees. Scientists are developing and testing another variety of chestnut tree that they hope will be resistant to the disease.

River Otter

These mammals live throughout Virginia. They are most common in coastal areas and on the lower parts of rivers and streams. River otters usually have brown fur with patches of silvery gray, a long tail, and short legs. They move comfortably on land but spend most of their time in the river. Their webbed feet help them move swiftly through the water. River otters eat turtles, fish, and frogs.

Bluefish

These fish can range in size from 12 to 36 inches (30 to 90 cm). They are usually a bluish green with silvery areas. Bluefish thrive along Virginia's Atlantic coast and in Chesapeake Bay. They usually travel in large schools and eat squid and smaller fish.

Chincoteague Pony

These small horses actually live on Assateague Island, a barrier island separated from Chincoteague by a narrow channel. According to one legend, the ponies are descended from a herd that survived the wreck of a Spanish ship in the 1500s. However, the herds are more likely descended from horses that the early settlers brought over to the island to graze.

2

From the Beginning

The history of Virginia stretches back further than that of any other state. It started out as the first permanent English colony established in the Americas. The history of the land goes back even deeper into the past.

The First Inhabitants

Scientists have established that humans moved into the area now known as Virginia about 16,000 years ago. By about 1400 CE, the descendants of those early people were part of the Woodland American Indian culture that existed throughout the East.

The American Indians who first met Europeans on Virginia's Atlantic coast belonged to groups that spoke Algonquian languages. In the early 1600s, as many as 50,000 American Indians were living in the region. They had semipermanent villages and moved every few years for fresh land to grow their crops. Their homes were longhouses called *yehakins*. They were made of bark

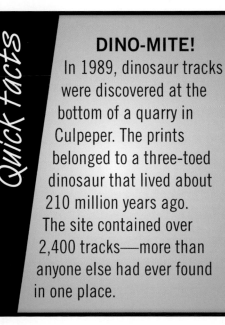

Quick Facts

DINO-MITE!

In 1989, dinosaur tracks were discovered at the bottom of a quarry in Culpeper. The prints belonged to a three-toed dinosaur that lived about 210 million years ago. The site contained over 2,400 tracks—more than anyone else had ever found in one place.

Children visiting Jamestown Settlement, a living-history museum of early America, dress in costume.

This illustration shows English ships en route to what is now Virginia in the late sixteenth century.

or reeds stretched over a frame of wooden poles. These Indians grew a variety of crops unknown to Europeans, including corn, beans, squash, and sunflowers. They also used nets to catch fish from Chesapeake Bay.

The Arrival of Europeans

In the late 1500s, English explorer Sir Walter Raleigh hoped to start a colony in North America. He planned to call the region Virginia, in honor of England's ruler Elizabeth I, known as the "Virgin Queen." Unlike the pilgrims who traveled to Massachusetts a few decades later, the people bound for Virginia were not looking for religious freedom. They wanted economic opportunity.

Raleigh's first attempt at colonization occurred in 1585 on the island of Roanoke. Life was hard for the settlers, who nearly starved to death. They abandoned the region in 1586, but Raleigh tried again in 1587. Governor John White led the second group to land on Roanoke. He soon went back to England for supplies. When White returned in 1590, he found the settlement empty and no trace of his people. No one knows for sure what happened to the settlers.

In 1606, a group called the Virginia Company received a charter, or contract, from King James of England to establish a colony in Virginia. In May 1607, three ships—the *Susan Constant*, *Godspeed*, and *Discovery*—dropped anchor in a waterway they named the James River. More than one hundred men and boys established the fortified village of Jamestown. In the first years, more than half the colonists died of disease and starvation.

The Jamestown colony survived largely because Captain John Smith took charge. He insisted that every man work and persuaded the nearby American Indians, called Powhatans, to help with planting crops. By this time, there were more than 150 Powhatan villages in what is now Virginia. The Indians' chief, Wahunsenacawh (later known simply as Powhatan), had mixed feelings about the settlers. He knew the Europeans could be dangerous, but he also recognized the value of trading with them. For a while, the two groups worked together.

After injuries forced Smith to go back to England, the colony again experienced a "starving time." In spite of these difficulties, more settlers came with more supplies.

Then, around 1612, settler John Rolfe discovered that tobacco grew well in Virginia's climate and could be sold for great profit in England. Settlers

The first settlers from England give thanks for a safe arrival at Jamestown.

THE STORY OF POCAHONTAS

English captain John Smith told of a story in which the Powhatans took him prisoner. They were about to execute him when Chief Powhatan's young daughter, Pocahontas, persuaded her father to spare Smith. While historians are not sure if this account is true, they do know that Pocahontas married English settler John Rolfe and went with him to England. There, people treated her like royalty and called her Princess Rebecca. Pocahontas was going to return to Virginia when she became ill and died.

began growing tobacco everywhere. They rushed to take more and more land from the Indians. Powhatan grew angry when he realized the English had come "not for trade but to invade my people and possess my country." Tensions between the American Indians and the settlers grew.

Growing Pains

The tobacco trade strained relations between the American Indians and the colonists. In time, this trade led to suffering for another group—enslaved African Americans. Tobacco profits helped make the Virginia colony a success and the colonists who established plantations rich. At first, the planters hired indentured servants from England to work the fields. An indentured servant signed a contract, or indenture, to work for someone, usually for seven years. In return, that person paid for the servant's trip across the ocean. Many workers signed up as indentured servants, hoping to start new lives in the new land after their years of service were over.

In 1619, a Dutch ship brought the first Africans to Virginia. Many other ships carrying Africans who had been captured and forcibly removed from their homeland soon followed. At first, at least some of the Africans were considered indentured servants. By 1661, however, laws were passed declaring that the new arrivals from Africa were "bound for life." Slavery was official.

As the Virginia colony prospered and grew, land-hungry settlers pushed further onto Powhatan lands. In the early 1620s, the American Indians fought back, killing about 350 settlers. In 1624, the English king, Charles I, canceled the Virginia Company's charter and made Virginia America's first royal colony. He also appointed a governor.

More settlers came to the area, and by 1700, practically all trace of the Algonquian people was gone. Wars and disease had wiped out many of them. The surviving American Indians had either given up their traditional ways of life to join white society or moved west beyond the mountains.

A Thriving and Independent Colony

By the 1770s, Virginia was a thriving colony of about 120,000 people. Many families lived on small farms, but the wealthy plantation owners dominated the economy, social life, and government.

Through the 1600s and 1700s, Virginians had become accustomed to governing themselves. In 1619, for example, they established their own legislature, or law-making body. This legislature, called the House of Burgesses, was one of the first steps toward self-government and democracy in America.

In 1676, when the royal governor tried to establish tighter control, a colonist named Nathaniel Bacon led an uprising against him. The uprising, called Bacon's Rebellion, did not last long, but it revealed an independent colonial spirit almost one hundred years before the American Revolution.

By the 1750s, some bold pioneers had pushed beyond the mountains into the Ohio River Valley, where they ran into fierce opposition from American Indians. The French, who had established a colony in present-day Canada, supported the Indians. The French were also interested in establishing forts and fur-trading outposts in the Ohio Valley. In 1754, George Washington, then a lieutenant colonel in the Virginia militia, led a group of militiamen to establish a fort in what is now western Pennsylvania. Washington and his men were forced back by the French. That incident was the start of a long war in which Britain, with the help of the Thirteen Colonies and some Indian allies, fought against France and its Indian allies.

Known as the French and Indian War, the conflict ended in 1763 with a British victory. As a result, France lost to Great Britain virtually all the land it had colonized or claimed in North America east of the Mississippi River.

Taxing the Colonies

Great Britain needed money to pay for the war—and to govern its huge empire—so King George III decided to tax the American colonies. Many colonists were very angry. Any taxes in the past had always been voted on by each colony's legislature, such as Virginia's House of Burgesses. Since the colonists had no representatives in the British legislature, or Parliament, their rallying cry became "No taxation without representation!"

The protests, led by colonists who called themselves patriots, continued from the 1760s to 1775. A lot of the action occurred in New England. The Boston Massacre, a skirmish in which British soldiers shot five colonists, took place in 1770. In the Boston Tea Party, colonists protested the British tax on tea by throwing chests of tea from British ships. However, patriots from farther south were doing their part for the movement, as well.

In September 1774, the First Continental Congress met in Philadelphia. It had delegates from twelve of the thirteen colonies, including Virginia. At the time, delegates hoped to settle their problems with Great Britain peacefully. They were not intent on independence. Delegates from Virginia included George Washington, Patrick Henry, and Peyton Randolph. Randolph was elected president of the Congress.

In March 1775, the Virginia governor suspended the House of Burgesses. Many representatives continued to meet in a church. At one meeting, patriot

Patrick Henry gives his famous "Give me liberty, or give me death!" speech to the Virginia Assembly in 1775.

Patrick Henry delivered a passionate speech, urging the representatives to take up arms against Britain in self-defense. He ended with the ringing challenge, "I know not what course others may take; but as for me, give me liberty, or give me death!" One month later, fighting broke out at the battles of Lexington and Concord in Massachusetts. When news came of these conflicts, Virginia patriots were ready to fight for independence.

The Fight for Independence

Soon after the outbreak of war, the Second Continental Congress began meeting in Philadelphia in May 1775. Over the months that followed, the Congress made several important decisions. It named George Washington commander of the Continental Army. The delegates also discussed whether they should declare independence from Britain. In June 1776, Virginia delegate and lawyer Richard Henry Lee introduced a resolution asking the Congress to vote for independence.

Another Virginia delegate, Thomas Jefferson, made a great contribution to history and the future. He became the main author of the Declaration of Independence. One of the celebrated documents of American democracy, the declaration stated, in clear and eloquent language, the principles that all people are entitled to freedom and equal treatment and that government should serve the people. Based on these principles, the declaration went on to give the reasons why the Thirteen Colonies deserved to be free and independent states. The Congress voted in favor of Lee's resolution on July 2, and it accepted the Declaration of Independence on July 4, 1776.

Of course, George Washington was also vital to the patriots' cause. When his ill-equipped, half-starved army was reduced to a few hundred men, Washington managed to inspire the patriots' hopes. In 1781, Washington and his men trapped the main British army at Yorktown, Virginia. The battered British were finally forced to surrender, though the war was not officially over until the signing of the Treaty of Paris in 1783.

A New Constitution

The Americans had won their independence. They finally achieved a stable government when representatives met in Philadelphia in 1787 to write a new constitution for the new nation. James Madison, a representative from Virginia, played a key role in creating the document that established the structure and powers of the U.S. government.

The U.S. Constitution was officially approved, or ratified, in 1788. Many Americans, including Patrick Henry, had opposed the Constitution because they feared a national government that might become too powerful. A handful of patriots, including Madison and Virginian John Marshall, wrote brilliant essays defending the Constitution. That helped persuade enough states to ratify it. Many historians feel that another encouraging factor was George Washington's willingness to serve as the new nation's first president.

General George Washington fires the first shot at Yorktown, Virginia, in 1781. The Battle of Yorktown, a decisive patriot victory, helped end the American Revolution.

MAKING A "HISTORICAL" DOCUMENT

As paper ages, it can turn brown and fall apart. That is why historic documents such as the Declaration of Independence and the Constitution look the way they do. By following these directions, you can create a document that looks hundreds of years old.

Hundreds of years ago, people used quills—or feathers—as pens. You can make your own quill pen and then use the pen to write your historical document. Be sure to ask an adult for help with this project.

To make a quill pen, you will need:

One feather (available at craft stores)

Utility knife

Small, sharp scissors

Have an adult help you with this part of the project because the blade is sharp. Use the knife to cut the tip of the quill at a sharp angle. Cut away about 1/2 to 1 inch (1.25 to 2.5 cm). On the long side of the quill point, carefully make a 1/2-inch slit down the center. Use the scissors to cut a curve on each side of the slit.

To make old-looking paper, you will need:

Plain white notebook-size paper

1 tea bag

Large bowl

Fill the bowl almost to the top with hot water. Add the tea bag and let it sit for 10 minutes. Carefully remove the tea bag from the dark brown water. Crumple the paper into a ball and put it in the bowl of tea.

After the water has cooled, remove the paper and let it dry completely. If the paper is not brown enough, repeat the process. You can lightly tear the edges or use scissors to create jagged edges to make the paper look older.

Once you are ready, use your quill pen to write a story or poem, draw a picture, or sign your name. You can dip your pen in dark ink or paint. When you are done, wash your quill pen with warm soapy water. Let your document dry completely before handling it.

Division and War

In the years following independence, Americans wrestled with the basic question of slavery. How could Americans believe in the ideal that "all men are created equal," as Jefferson had written in the Declaration of Independence, yet still allow slavery—the ownership of other human beings? By the 1820s, most of the states in the North had outlawed, or abolished, slavery. In the South, however, where the plantations needed cheap or free labor, slavery was considered a necessary part of life.

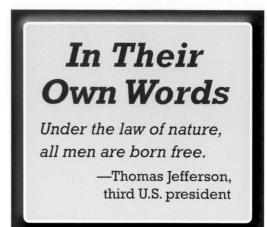

There were also Southerners, including plantation owners, who felt that slavery was wrong, though that did not stop many from keeping their slaves. For some, the decision was purely economic—they could not afford to run their plantations without slave labor. George Washington was one planter who arranged to have his slaves freed after his death. Though he struggled with the question of slavery, Jefferson could not find a solution.

Between 1820 and 1860, the North and the South drifted further apart. Many Virginians, and others in the South, felt that the North was beginning to dominate the nation's economy and government. It seemed that the North's power threatened not just slavery but their entire way of life.

Quick Facts

NAT TURNER'S REBELLION

One of America's largest slave uprisings took place in Virginia in August 1831. More than forty slaves, led by an enslaved man named Nat Turner, killed fifty-five white people. Many of the rebels, including Turner, were eventually caught and put to death. In the aftermath, white mobs murdered almost two hundred black people, most of whom had nothing to do with the rebellion.

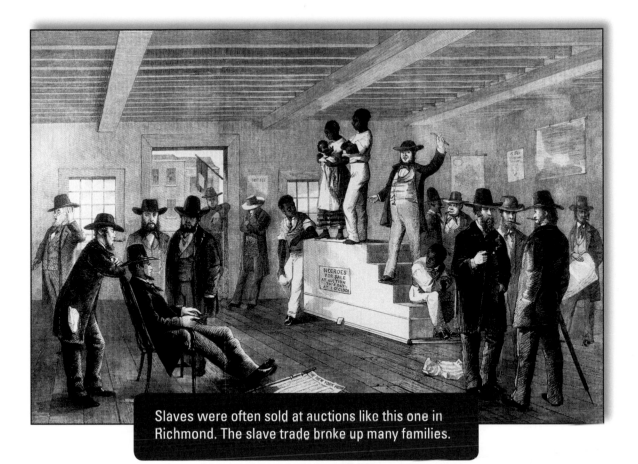

Slaves were often sold at auctions like this one in Richmond. The slave trade broke up many families.

When Abraham Lincoln was elected president in 1860, many Southerners were convinced that the government would force the end of slavery. At first, seven Southern states—Alabama, Florida, Georgia, Louisiana, Mississippi, South Carolina, and Texas—decided to secede from, or leave, the Union (the United States). They formed an independent nation, the Confederate States of America, which is also known as the Confederacy.

The people of Virginia were not sure what they should do. They decided not to leave the Union unless war between the North and South was unavoidable. Confederate forces attacked Fort Sumter in South Carolina in April 1861. President Lincoln then called for volunteers to join the army and fight to reunite the Union. Virginia, along with Arkansas, North Carolina, and Tennessee, decided to join the Confederacy. Richmond was named the capital of the Confederate States of America soon after.

General Robert E. Lee was just one Virginian who struggled with the problem of divided loyalties. Although Lee was a member of Virginia's planter class, he hated slavery. He also believed secession was unconstitutional. A member of the U.S. military, Lee had graduated second in his class from the U.S. Military Academy at West Point. He was a brave and well-respected soldier. By the time the Civil War broke out, Lee had been named the superintendent of West Point. However, when Lee was offered command of the Union armies, he resigned from the army. He could not bring himself to fight against his native state. Lee joined the Confederate army and became its greatest general.

The people of Virginia's northwestern counties refused to accept the state's decision. They voted to break away and form the separate state of West Virginia. West Virginia entered the Union in 1863.

Many people believed the war would end quickly in victory for the Union. After all, the North had a larger population than the South and housed three-quarters of the nation's factories and railroads. Southerners, however, believed they were fighting for their way of life and their homes. Many soldiers did not even own slaves. They felt they were fighting off invaders who had attacked their country. The South also had a well-trained cavalry and a number of outstanding generals, many of them Virginians. In fact, the South relied heavily on Virginia because the state had about half the South's weapons factories and railroads.

The war lasted four long, bloody years, from 1861 to 1865. Virginia paid a heavy price for its leadership of the Confederacy. Because the Confederate capital was located in Richmond, many battles took place on Virginia soil.

In Their Own Words

With all my devotion to the Union, and the feeling of loyalty and duty of an American citizen, I have not been able to make up my mind to raise my hand against my relatives, my children, my home.

—Virginian and Confederate general Robert E. Lee

Union soldiers attack Confederate cavalrymen at the First Battle of Bull Run on July 21, 1861. It was the first major land battle of the American Civil War.

More than one hundred battles—one-third of all the fighting—occurred there. Thousands of the state's young men were killed and thousands more crippled. In all, the Civil War claimed more than 600,000 lives. When the war did end in a victory for the North, the states of the Confederacy were brought back into the Union, and slavery was finally abolished throughout the United States, setting 4 million people free.

The Modern Age

Much of Virginia's story from the late nineteenth century to the early twenty-first century involves the emergence of modern industries and the development of urban and suburban areas. At the end of the nineteenth century, Virginia had many farming communities and few large cities. Today's Virginia has a small percentage of farming families and many people living in cities or suburbs.

A mechanical reaper invented by Virginian Cyrus McCormick harvests wheat.

These great changes, shared by all the states, were the result of the Industrial Revolution of the nineteenth century. Machines now performed work that, in the past, had depended on human or animal power. In the early 1830s, for example, Virginian Cyrus McCormick invented a mechanical reaper for harvesting wheat. By 1900, McCormick's machines, pulled by tractors, enabled farmers to harvest enormous wheat fields in a single day. Machines allowed farmers to produce more crops with fewer workers.

Inventions like McCormick's created new industries and new ways of working and living. By the early 1900s, automobiles, electric lights, and telephones contributed to the amazing changes in American life.

Textile mills (factories where cloth was made), long an important part of Virginia's economy, remained important through the early 1900s. New machines helped mills become more productive, but they still required human operators. Unfortunately, the working conditions in these mills were often very bad. Children, men, and women worked long hours for low pay in dark, cramped rooms with little fresh air. In the early 1900s, laws were passed to protect workers and improve conditions in textile mills and other factories.

The Great Depression and Beyond

From 1929 through the 1930s, the entire country suffered through the severe economic times known as the Great Depression. People across the country lost their jobs, their homes, and their belongings. At the height of the depression, almost 13 million people—one-quarter of the nation's workforce—were unemployed.

The government, under President Franklin D. Roosevelt, established programs to help those Americans who needed it most. One program was the Civilian Conservation Corps (CCC). This program employed men to work on highways and bridges and in forests. Many Virginians took part in the CCC. Hundreds of workers from Virginia and other states went into areas such as the Blue Ridge to harvest lumber or create camping areas and hiking trails.

The start of World War II in 1939 also eased some of the effects of the Great Depression. American factories were put to work, at first making weapons and

Civilian Conservation Corps recruits arrive to set up a work camp to preserve natural resources in 1933.

THE PENTAGON

Construction on the Pentagon started on September 11, 1941. When it was finished, the Pentagon was the country's largest office building, and at its peak, it housed almost 33,000 workers. On September 11, 2001—exactly sixty years after the groundbreaking ceremony—a hijacked airplane hit the Pentagon, killing more than one hundred people inside.

Virginia is home to the Pentagon, the headquarters of the nation's Department of Defense.

equipment for countries in Europe that the United States was helping. When the United States joined the war after Japan bombed the U.S. naval base at Pearl Harbor, Hawaii, in 1941, even more weapons and supplies were needed to support the troops. Virginia's farms and factories produced many wartime supplies. Americans found work in these now-busy factories. Women were encouraged to work in the factories because many men were fighting in the war.

Since World War II, growth and change have continued to characterize life in Virginia. Coastal cities such as Hampton, Newport News, and Virginia Beach have become major population centers. Cities on the western edge of the Piedmont, such as Charlottesville and Roanoke, have also grown. As the federal government has increased in size, more government offices have been located in northeastern Virginia, near Washington, D.C., and more people who have jobs in or related to the government have chosen to live in that area. While this growth has been occurring, though, the people of Virginia are determined to preserve the state's natural beauty and historic sites.

Important Dates

★ **1400** CE More than thirty Algonquian-speaking tribes inhabit the Tidewater region.

★ **1585** English explorer Sir Walter Raleigh tries to establish a colony on Roanoke Island.

★ **1587** Raleigh tries to set up a second Roanoke colony.

★ **1607** The Virginia Company of London founds Jamestown.

★ **1619** The House of Burgesses becomes the first law-making body in the Americas. The first Africans are forcibly brought to Virginia.

★ **1624** Virginia becomes a royal colony.

★ **1754–1763** The French and Indian War is fought.

★ **1775** The American Revolution begins.

★ **1776** Virginia declares its independence and adopts its first constitution. Thomas Jefferson writes the Declaration of Independence.

★ **1781** British troops surrender at Yorktown in Virginia. Two years later, the American Revolution officially ends.

★ **1788** Virginia becomes the tenth state to ratify the new U.S. Constitution.

★ **1789** George Washington takes office as the nation's first president.

★ **1861** The Civil War begins, and Virginia joins the Confederacy.

★ **1865** The Civil War ends.

★ **1881** Virginian Booker T. Washington founds Tuskegee Institute (now Tuskegee University).

★ **1939–1945** World War II is fought.

★ **1959** Prince Edward County closes its public schools to protest integration.

★ **1990** L. Douglas Wilder of Virginia becomes the first black U.S. governor.

★ **2001** Terrorists fly a hijacked airplane into the Pentagon.

★ **2007** The 400th anniversary of the Jamestown colony is celebrated.

The People

Some areas of Virginia, especially its urban areas, reflect the country's great mix of peoples and cultures from all parts of the world. In some geographic pockets of the state, however, there is very little diversity. Small communities on some of the Chesapeake Bay and offshore islands remained isolated from the 1600s to the late 1900s. The Chesapeake island of Tangier, for instance, is accessible only by boat or plane. The people there speak in a dialect unique to the area. For example, islanders pronounce *bank* as "bay-eenk." For *chair* and *scared*, they say "churr" and "scurred."

Diversity

The first European settlers in Virginia came from England, and a number of families are still considered FFVs—First Families of Virginia. The Byrd family, for example, established one of the first plantations in the 1600s. Family members have played an important part in the governments of Virginia and West Virginia ever since.

In the 1700s, colonists from other parts of the British Isles and Europe settled mostly in the Tidewater and the Piedmont regions. Farther west, hardy pioneers from Scotland and Ireland made their way south along the Appalachians and settled in the foothills of the Alleghenies and the Blue Ridge Mountains. Like some of the people living on Virginia's eastern islands, several hundred families

Pumpkins are native to Virginia and the Americas, but the ancestors of most of Virginia's population originated in other countries.

At milepost 176.2 of the Blue Ridge Parkway, visitors can watch woodworking, weaving, and blacksmith demonstrations at Mabry Mill.

became isolated in the mountain valleys. As a result, they developed their own crafts, making furniture, baskets, quilts, and musical instruments.

Throughout much of Virginia's history, people of African descent were largely isolated from the rest of the population. At the time of the Civil War, African Americans made up about 50 percent of the state's population. After 1865, that percentage steadily declined, as thousands of freed slaves headed north and west to look for jobs. The migration slowed in the late 1900s, however. Today, African Americans make up almost 20 percent of the state's population. The proportion of African Americans in the population varies within the state.

Many Virginians today say there are few signs of racial tension between white people and African Americans in spite of the state's history. When the civil rights movement began in the late 1950s, however, some incidents showed that not all Virginians were willing to accept an integrated society. When an African diplomat was refused a room in Virginia hotels because of his race, newspapers around the world reported the story. And in 1959, administrators closed public schools in Prince Edward County for five years because they did not want African-American children to attend. Since then, Virginia, like many other states in the country, has made many positive changes, including electing African Americans to local and statewide political offices.

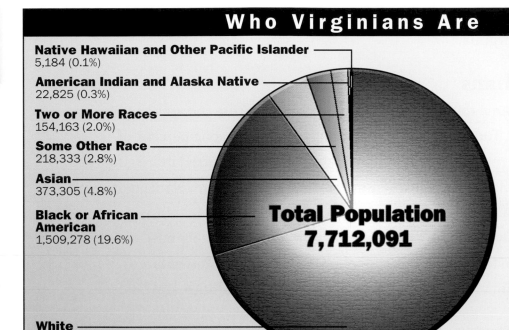

Who Virginians Are

Native Hawaiian and Other Pacific Islander
5,184 (0.1%)

American Indian and Alaska Native
22,825 (0.3%)

Two or More Races
154,163 (2.0%)

Some Other Race
218,333 (2.8%)

Asian
373,305 (4.8%)

Black or African American
1,509,278 (19.6%)

White
5,429,003 (70.4%)

Total Population 7,712,091

Hispanics or Latinos:
- 500,707 people
- 6.5% of the state's population

Hispanics or Latinos may be of any race.

Note: The pie chart shows the racial breakdown of the state's population based on the categories used by the U.S. Bureau of the Census. The Census Bureau reports information for Hispanics or Latinos separately, since they may be of any race. Percentages in the pie chart may not add to 100 because of rounding.

Source: U.S. Bureau of the Census, 2007 American Community Survey

Over the past thirty or forty years, Virginia's population has changed to include more people from different parts of the world than ever before. Immigrants come to Virginia from China, Japan, India, and other parts of Asia. There has also been an increase in Hispanic residents from Mexico, the

These children are enjoying an open-air fountain at a shopping district in Newport News.

Caribbean, and Central and South America. These groups have added a cultural richness to life in Virginia.

American Indians

Before Europeans came to the region, American Indians were the area's only human inhabitants. Today, however, they make up less than one percent of the population. Currently, there are eight tribal groups recognized in Virginia: the Chickahominy, Eastern Chickahominy, Mattaponi, Monacan, Nansemond, Pamunkey, Rappahannock, and Upper Mattaponi.

The state has only two reservations—one is occupied by the Pamunkeys and the other by the Mattaponis. Both groups are part of the Powhatan Confederacy. The Monacans recently won ownership of their ancestral lands on Bear Mountain.

The Pamunkey reservation is on the Pamunkey River. It includes about 1,200 acres (490 ha) of land. Almost thirty families live on the reservation. Other Pamunkeys live in nearby cities and towns. There used to be a Pamunkey school on the reservation, but now most Pamunkey children attend the public schools in King William County. The Pamunkeys have their own tribal government made up of a chief and seven council members. Elections are held every four years. The tribal government is responsible for upholding the laws that the Pamunkeys have established.

The reservation also includes the Pamunkey Indian Museum, which documents and celebrates the Pamunkeys' history in the state. These Indians are well known for their pottery, beadwork, and other art. They sell some of their impressive artwork to support the community, but most is created to honor Pamunkey traditions.

Quick Facts

EARLY THANKSGIVING
In 1646, the Mattaponis paid tribute to the Virginia governor. This old tradition continues today. Every year, on the fourth Wednesday of November, the tribe gives a gift of fish or game to the governor of the commonwealth.

Mattaponis in traditional dress perform at a powwow on the Mattaponi Indian Reservation in Westpoint.

The Mattaponis trace their heritage directly to Powhatan, the great chief and father of Pocahontas. The Mattaponi reservation, one of the oldest in the country, was established in 1658. Located near the Mattaponi River, it covers about 150 acres (60 ha). More than four hundred people are officially part of the Mattaponi tribe, but fewer than a quarter of them live on the reservation. The Mattaponis also have their own government, including a chief, an assistant chief, and seven council members.

The reservation houses a fish hatchery and marine science center. The American shad is a fish important to the Mattaponis' diet and culture. At the center, Mattaponis monitor shad populations and water quality. They also develop educational resources that help communities protect their land and water.

Education in Virginia

Education is an important issue for many Virginians. The state has been one of the nation's leaders in higher education. For example, the College of William and Mary, founded in Williamsburg in 1693, is the country's second-oldest college. In 1819, the University of Virginia was established in Charlottesville, largely thanks to the work of Thomas Jefferson. The Virginia Military Institute, founded in 1839, is the nation's oldest state-supported military college. In 1868, the Hampton Normal and Agricultural Institute (now Hampton University) was created to prepare African-American men and women to teach newly freed people.

Virginia's public schools for elementary and secondary school children, however, did not develop as early or as quickly. A law establishing public schools in Virginia was not passed until 1846—two hundred years after Massachusetts

Sixteen signers of the Declaration of Independence attended the College of William and Mary in Williamsburg.

Virginia's public schools are working to improve their educational system on all levels.

passed a similar law. Even then, the Virginia law was not strongly enforced. There were various reasons for this lack of interest in public education. Until the Civil War era, plantation owners hired tutors for their children or operated small schools for local white children. Local church congregations also established their own schools. Over time, however, Virginia did establish public school systems throughout the state.

In the 1960s, studies showed that Virginia's public schools ranked below the national average. Educators and parents worked to raise the schools' rankings. They formed committees to improve courses and pressed the state government for money to modernize facilities and increase pay for teachers. The determination of educators, parents, students, and legislators has paid off. According to the National Center for Education Statistics, Virginia's math and reading scores beat the national average every year from 1992 to 2009. While there is still more to do, this one example shows how Virginians can work together to improve their state.

Calendar of Events

★ **George Washington Birthday Celebration**

Since the time of the American Revolution, people in Alexandria have been celebrating George Washington's birthday. Every February, they mark the occasion with reenactments of historic events, parades, music, and balls. Celebrations also take place at Washington's home, Mount Vernon, a few miles down the Potomac River.

★ **Historic Garden Week**

When flowers and plants are in bloom in April, gardens throughout the state are open to the public, with tours of gardens in many private homes as well as in historic homes.

★ **Shenandoah Apple Blossom Festival**

Every April, more than 250,000 people flock to the Shenandoah Valley to take part in a festival that includes everything from band competitions to a circus.

★ **Reenactment of the Battle of New Market**

In May, volunteers, including many teens, reenact the 1864 Civil War battle in which cadets from the nearby Virginia Military Institute in Lexington fought against Union soldiers. The reenactment occurs on the battle site, which is part of a state historic park. The park also includes living-history presentations that offer a glimpse of life for Confederate soldiers.

★ **Hampton Jazz Festival**

This festival, held the last full weekend in June, features outstanding jazz bands, as well as craft displays and food.

★ Mattaponi Indian Reservation Powwow

Every June, the Mattaponis hold their annual powwow—the only one in Virginia that takes place on a reservation. The celebration features American Indian dancing, drumming, food, and arts and crafts.

★ Virginia Highlands Festival

This July event at the Shenandoah town of Abingdon was originally created to preserve and celebrate the cultural heritage of the highlands area. Over the past sixty years, the festival has grown to represent all of southwest Virginia through traditional music, crafts, and food.

★ Harborfest

Held in Norfolk each July, Harborfest is one of the Atlantic Coast's largest waterfront festivals. Visitors gather to see the ships and celebrate the state's nautical history. The event features musical performances, food, shopping, and fireworks.

★ State Fair of Virginia

The state fair, which lasts for a little more than a week at the end of September, has been an annual tradition since 1854. The festivities include games, musical performances, antiques, and arts and crafts, as well as animals and agricultural exhibits.

★ Grand Illumination

Every December, Colonial Williamsburg celebrates the holiday season with a festival of lights. Historic homes are lit up and decorated as they might have been in the 1700s. There is also a fireworks display and traditional fife and drum music.

4

How the Government Works

On June 29, 1776, Virginia became an independent commonwealth when its representatives adopted its first constitution. The constitution established an executive branch, two legislative houses, and a judicial department. The most important part of the constitution, however, was its Declaration of Rights. Many of the ideas in Virginia's constitution later made their way into the U.S. Constitution. Today, Virginia is one of four states that officially call themselves commonwealths (the others are Kentucky, Massachusetts, and Pennsylvania). The word

FATHER OF THE BILL OF RIGHTS

George Mason wrote much of the Virginia constitution, including the Declaration of Rights, in 1776. Mason, a representative at the 1787 convention at which the U.S. Constitution was written, worried about giving too much power to the federal government. He successfully argued to add a Bill of Rights. The first ten amendments to the U.S. Constitution, called the Bill of Rights, guarantee Americans important freedoms, including the freedoms of speech and religion. They also give Americans protection from unfair treatment by the government. Mason's efforts earned him the nickname Father of the Bill of Rights.

The Virginia State Capitol is located in Richmond.

Branches of Government

EXECUTIVE ★ ★ ★ ★ ★ ★ ★ ★

The governor, lieutenant governor, and state attorney general are elected for four-year terms. The governor's major job is to see that the laws are carried out. He or she appoints the directors of executive departments, such as education and transportation, who oversee the day-to-day work of the government. The governor can also propose new laws and can reject laws passed by the general assembly. Virginia is the only state in which the governor cannot serve two consecutive terms.

LEGISLATIVE ★ ★ ★ ★ ★ ★ ★ ★

The law-making body is the general assembly, made up of two houses—a forty-member senate, elected for four-year terms, and a house of delegates, with one hundred members elected for two-year terms.

JUDICIAL ★ ★ ★ ★ ★ ★ ★ ★

There are four levels of courts. The Virginia supreme court with its seven judges is the highest state court. The state supreme court hears appeals of decisions made by the lower courts. Below the supreme court is the court of appeals. Below that are the thirty-one judicial circuits that deal with general court matters, trying both criminal cases and civil cases, in which someone seeks damages from a company or an individual. The fourth—and lowest—level is made up of special courts, such as juvenile courts or family courts.

commonwealth can mean a group of people who join together for the common good.

Throughout the state's history, Virginians have been willing to make changes to their government when needed. The 1776 state constitution has gone through five major revisions. Other changes have been achieved by a simple act of the general assembly (the state legislature). In colonial times, for example, the Episcopal Church was the state's official church, but many people felt this was not fair to those who followed other religions or no religion. Thomas Jefferson devised a new law, the Virginia Statute for Religious Freedom, that guaranteed freedom of worship for all. Jefferson's law has been a model for other state constitutions.

A more recent example of how Virginia alters its government to accommodate changing times relates to the state supreme court. The general assembly appointed a commission to look for ways to help the Virginia supreme court because the sheer number of cases was overwhelming the court. The state legislators suggested adding another court to hear appeals (requests for a court decision to be reviewed). This court of appeals would decide some of the cases. The supreme court would get the cases that involved a more complicated interpretation of the state constitution. The new court, called the court of appeals, went into effect in 1985. It has helped relieve the pressure on the state's highest court.

Government of the People

Most Virginians believe that the structure of their government should be as simple as possible to respond to the needs of the people. To bring government close to the people, the voters in each of the ninety-five counties elect a board of supervisors to handle most local matters. Each town sends a supervisor to the county board. There are thirty-nine cities, which are usually governed by a mayor and city council. In Virginia, cities are independent from counties.

All levels of the Virginia government work to help businesses. The Department of Economic Development, for example, which operates out of the governor's office, works with business groups to attract new opportunities to the state.

The state government serves a similar function for the arts. This involvement began in 1936, during the Great Depression. To help

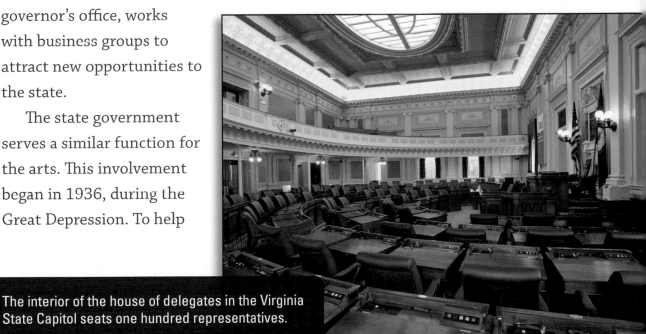

The interior of the house of delegates in the Virginia State Capitol seats one hundred representatives.

the many artists who were out of work, the general assembly created the Virginia Museum of the Fine Arts—the country's first state-supported museum of the arts. The museum provided a place for artists to display their work. It also established a performing arts program, providing funds to support performances by local theater groups, symphony orchestras, and dance companies.

In addition to state and local government, Virginia is represented in the U.S. Congress in Washington, D.C. Like all other states, Virginia has two U.S. senators who serve six-year terms. As of 2010, the state had eleven representatives in the U.S. House of Representatives. Representatives serve two-year terms. A state's population determines its number of representatives.

How a Bill Becomes a Law

As in other states, before a law is passed in Virginia, it goes through an established process. Most laws begin with a suggestion or an idea from a Virginia resident or a member of the state legislature. The proposed law is called a bill.

When a bill is introduced by a legislator in one of the two legislative houses, it is assigned to a committee. The committee members examine the bill, hold meetings or hearings, and may revise the bill. The committee can reject the bill and decide not to take it any further. But if the committee is satisfied with the bill, it presents the bill to the entire house.

The bill is read to the house three times. After the second reading, legislators can amend—or revise—the bill. They usually debate the bill after the third reading. Then the legislators vote on the bill. If it is approved, it is sent to the other house, where it goes through a similar process.

THE ROAD TO THE WHITE HOUSE

Another of Virginia's nicknames is the "Birthplace of Presidents." This is because eight U.S. presidents—including four of the first five—were Virginians: George Washington, Thomas Jefferson, James Madison, James Monroe, William Henry Harrison, John Tyler, Zachary Taylor, and Woodrow Wilson.

Several U.S. presidents, including (from left to right, carved into South Dakota's Mount Rushmore) George Washington and Thomas Jefferson, were Virginians. (Theodore Roosevelt and Abraham Lincoln are to the right.)

If both houses agree on the bill, it is sent to the governor. If the governor approves the bill, he or she can sign it into law. The governor can also make changes to the bill and send it back to the general assembly. If the governor does not take any action, the bill will automatically become law after a certain amount of time. The governor can also veto—or reject—the bill. The vetoed bill can still become law if two-thirds of the members of both houses vote to override the governor's veto.

★ 5 ★
Making a Living

The mix of industries in Virginia reveals the same blending of old and new that exists in so much of the state's life. Some people work in traditional occupations such as farming and fishing. Others spend their time exploring Virginia's past by working at one of the many historic sites. Still others are engaged in manufacturing, research, or providing services. Service workers include people in a wide range of jobs, such as government employees, teachers, health-care workers, and staff at hotels, restaurants, and shops as well as all the tourist sites.

Agriculture

For much of Virginia's history, most families lived by farming. Today, far fewer people are engaged in agriculture. Still, the state has more than 47,000 farms on 8.5 million acres (3.4 million ha) of farmland. Almost 90 percent of the farms are family owned. The state has more than 1,000 "Century Farms"—farms in operation for one hundred years or more.

Soybeans were Virginia's number-one cash crop in 2008, bringing in more than $135 million in revenue. Soybeans are used in many products, including tofu, oil, soap, and crayons. Corn is the commonwealth's number-two cash crop. The corn grown there is used mostly for grain to feed livestock. Today, tobacco is Virginia's third most important cash crop.

Horseback riders stand in front of their barn in Virginia. Most of Virginia's farms are family owned.

Rockingham County in the Shenandoah Valley is one of the nation's largest turkey-raising centers. The state ranks fourth in the nation for turkey production. However, chickens are Virginia's most valuable agricultural product. In 2007, state poultry farms produced 1.3 billion pounds (590 million kg) of chicken, worth more than $559 million. Cattle also play an important role in Virginia's agricultural industry. Beef is the second-largest commodity in the state, and milk is the third.

Virginia is also well known for its horse farms in the northwestern part of the state. In fact, Triple Crown winner Secretariat was born in Doswell. Home to 170,000 horses, Virginia is the fifth-largest equine state in the nation.

Virginia grows many different kinds of fruits, including apples.

RECIPE FOR APPLE PUDDING

Apples are grown throughout the state. Certain types of apples, such as the Albemarle pippin, are popular, but you can use almost any type of apple for this recipe.

WHAT YOU NEED

2 cups (about $\frac{1}{2}$ liter) apples, peeled and chopped

1 teaspoon (5 grams) cinnamon

$1\frac{1}{4}$ cups (250 g) granulated sugar

$1\frac{1}{4}$ cups (160 g) all-purpose flour

$1\frac{1}{4}$ cups (350 milliliters) milk

$\frac{1}{2}$ cup (113 g) butter, melted

2 teaspoons (9 g) baking powder

$\frac{1}{2}$ teaspoon (2.5 g) salt

$\frac{1}{2}$ teaspoon (2.5 ml) vanilla extract

Preheat the oven to 375 °F (190 °C).

Place the apples in a microwave-safe bowl. Add the cinnamon and stir to combine. Cook on HIGH for about 3 minutes, or until the apples are soft.

Meanwhile, mix together the sugar, flour, milk, butter, baking powder, salt, and vanilla in a baking dish. Stir until a smooth batter forms. Pour the apple mixture into the center of the batter.

Bake until golden, about 30 minutes. Ask an adult to help you place the pudding in the oven and take it out—the dish will be very hot. Let the pudding cool before serving. For a real treat, top it with a scoop of your favorite ice cream.

Gifts from the Sea and Bay

Since the earliest days of Jamestown, Virginians have relied on products from the Atlantic Ocean and Chesapeake Bay. Today, crab and oyster farms are scattered along the jagged shore of the bay. Shellfish, such as oysters, clams, and the famous blue crabs, are an important part of the commercial fishing industry. Flounder, bass (called rockfish in the Chesapeake region), and a number of other fish also thrive in Virginia waters. Offshore, many sea clams and scallops are harvested. Fishers catch large ocean fish, such as swordfish and tuna, on baited hooks pulled close to the surface. These fishing lines can be 40 to 50 miles (65 to 80 km) long!

One important type of fish is menhaden. The Algonquian Indians called it *munnawhatteaug*, which means "fertilizer." They used the menhaden to fertilize their crops—a technique they taught to the early settlers.

Today, people in small aircraft spot schools of

A young Virginian holds up a couple of blue crabs.

Fishers haul in a huge net full of menhaden near Reedville.

menhaden and radio the locations to fishing boats. Fishers then catch the menhaden in large nets. As in colonial times, people do not eat the fish but use it for fertilizer. People also feed menhaden to their livestock, make fishing bait out of it, and use its oil to produce food, paint, and cosmetics.

Workers & Industries

Industry	Number of People Working in That Industry	Percentage of All Workers Who Are Working in That Industry
Education and health care	747,072	19.7%
Professionals, scientists, and managers	525,438	13.9%
Wholesale and retail businesses	503,320	13.2%
Publishing, media, entertainment, hotels, and restaurants	390,280	10.3%
Government	343,682	9.1%
Manufacturing	308,832	8.1%
Construction	306,975	8.1%
Banking and finance, insurance, and real estate	262,164	6.9%
Other services	192,928	5.1%
Transportation and public utilities	163,987	4.3%
Farming, fishing, forestry, and mining	46,231	1.2%
Totals	3,790,909	100%

Notes: Figures above do not include people in the armed forces. "Professionals" includes people such as doctors and lawyers. Percentages may not add to 100 because of rounding.

Source: U.S. Bureau of the Census, 2007 estimates

A Changing Economy

The twentieth century saw major changes in Virginia's economic life. World War II, in particular, spurred the state's role in shipbuilding and in training bases for the military services. After the government hired the Newport News Shipbuilding and Dry Dock Company to build aircraft carriers and other warships for the U.S. Navy, it became the world's largest shipbuilding company.

Since parts of Virginia are very close to Washington, D.C., it is not surprising that the federal government is the employer of many Virginians. The headquarters for several government agencies are located in northern Virginia, including the Department of Defense (at the Pentagon), the U.S. Patent and Trademark Office, the U.S. Fish and Wildlife Service, the Central Intelligence Agency (CIA), and the National Science Foundation. Many Virginians commute to work in Washington, D.C.

A Wealth of Historic Sites

Visitors to Virginia can enjoy historical experiences at a number of magnificent plantations and the homes of famous Americans, including Washington's Mount Vernon and Jefferson's Monticello. Guests can tour the house that Thomas Jefferson designed and built for his family and enjoy the beautiful grounds of the Monticello estate. Jefferson's

Monticello is a popular attraction in the Virginia Piedmont.

talent as an architect is also on display in the buildings of the University of Virginia in Charlottesville and the Virginia State Capitol in Richmond.

In fact, no state in the nation has more historic sites than Virginia, including early homes, plantations, and battlefields dating from the American Revolution and the Civil War. Restoring and preserving these sites, along with providing guided tours and other services to visitors, adds to Virginia's tourism industry, which supports more than 200,000 jobs and generates almost $19 billion in spending. Some of the money people spend while visiting Virginia's sites, staying at hotels, eating at restaurants, and shopping in stores goes to the state government in the form of taxes.

Visitors to Colonial Williamsburg explore the homes and buildings where men such as Thomas Jefferson, George Washington, and Patrick Henry inspired the fight for independence.

COLONIAL WILLIAMSBURG

In 1926, a Virginia reverend named Dr. W. A. R Goodwin shared with American philanthropist John D. Rockefeller Jr. his dream of preserving Williamsburg's historic buildings. Rockefeller agreed that an important part of the nation's early history might soon be lost forever. He gave money to help restore and develop Colonial Williamsburg, which today encompasses about 85 percent of Virginia's original capital city. The site includes eighty-eight restored eighteenth-century structures as well as scores of reconstructed homes, shops, taverns, and government buildings.

Products & Resources

Apple Orchards

George Washington owned farmland in the Shenandoah Valley. According to legend, he required his tenants to plant 4 acres (1.6 ha) of apple trees on lands they leased from him. That was the beginning of the famous orchards around Winchester, which is known as Virginia's apple capital. Visitors come in the spring for the Shenandoah Apple Blossom Festival and again in autumn as different types of apples are ready for picking.

Military Centers

In addition to training military personnel, these facilities provide jobs for many Virginians. The major bases include Quantico, Norfolk Naval Base, Fort Eustis, and Fort Monroe. The Hampton–Newport News area has facilities for the U.S. Air Force and for the National Aeronautics and Space Administration (NASA). Yorktown is home to a U.S. Coast Guard base, a U.S. Naval Weapons Station, and a Naval Supply Center. Camp Peary Naval Reservation in Williamsburg is the headquarters for military intelligence training.

Virginia Peanuts

There are four basic types of peanuts: Runner, Virginia, Spanish, and Valencia. Each distinct type has a certain use. Virginia peanuts have the largest kernels and are best for roasting and snacking (as opposed to making peanut butter). In 2008, about 39,000 tons (35,000 metric tons) of peanuts were harvested in Virginia.

Civil War Battlefields

More than twenty battlefield sites from the Civil War add to Virginia's tourism industry. The most popular sites for visitors include Manassas—known to Northerners as Bull Run—where the Confederates won two victories, and the village of Appomattox Court House. It was there, at McClean House, that General Lee surrendered to Union general Grant. Many other sites are located between Washington, D.C., and Richmond and in the Shenandoah Valley.

Chesapeake Bay

Chesapeake Bay is one of the world's great spawning grounds for saltwater fish. Today the bay is a center for commercial and sport fishing. It is also a popular recreation site for boaters.

Smithfield Hams

The beautifully restored town of Smithfield is famous not only as a historic seaport but as the birthplace of the Smithfield hams. Produced by several companies, with slight variations, these hams are sold throughout the world.

Visiting Natural Wonders

Tourists also visit the state to enjoy its natural wonders. Many families enjoy camping in the state and national parks. The rivers, lakes, and streams offer great boating, swimming, and fishing. Many people go to Chesapeake Bay to enjoy the many water activities.

Virginia Beach is another popular tourist destination. It is said that this resort city has the longest pleasure beach in the world. Virginia Beach includes 35 miles (56 km) of waterfront property, a 3-mile (5-km) boardwalk, and plenty of entertainment, from restaurants and shops to live music. Birding trails, whale-watching expeditions, golf courses, and fishing competitions are other fun recreational offerings.

From its farms and waters to its historical sites and bustling cities, the Old Dominion is full of opportunities for Virginians and visitors. Virginia's economy draws strength from the land, the people, and their history.

Vacationers enjoy Virginia Beach, situated on the Atlantic Ocean and Chesapeake Bay.

State Flag & Seal

Virginia's flag is blue with the state seal in the center.

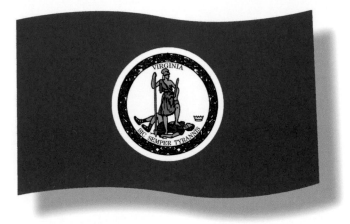

Virginia's state seal has two sides: a front and a back. The front shows Virtus, the Roman goddess of virtue, dressed as a warrior. She is standing with her left foot on the chest of a defeated warrior meant to represent tyranny. Virtus symbolizes the spirit of Virginia, and tyranny represents Great Britain. The bottom of the seal shows the state's motto. Translated from Latin, it means "Thus Always to Tyrants." The back of the seal shows three Roman goddesses representing liberty, eternity, and fruitfulness. They stand below the word Perservando, which means "by persevering."

BOOKS

Allen, Kathy. *President George Washington*. Mankato, MN: Picture Window Books, 2009.

Harkins, Susan S., and William H. Harkins. *Colonial Virginia*. Hockessin, DE: Mitchell Lane Publishers, 2007.

King, David C. *The Powhatan*. New York: Marshall Cavendish Benchmark, 2008.

Lange, Karen. *1607: A New Look at Jamestown*. Washington, DC: National Geographic Children's Books, 2007.

Miller, Lee. *Roanoke: The Mystery of the Lost Colony*. New York: Scholastic, 2007.

Trueit, Trudi Strain. *Thomas Jefferson*. New York: Marshall Cavendish Benchmark, 2009.

WEBSITES

Colonial Williamsburg:
http://www.colonialwilliamsburg.com

The Official Commonwealth of Virginia Home Page:
http://www.virginia.gov

The Official Tourism Website of the Commonwealth of Virginia:
http://www.virginia.org

David C. King is an award-winning author who has written more than forty books for children and young adults. He and his wife, Sharon, live in the Berkshires at the junction of New York, Massachusetts, and Connecticut. Their travels have taken them through most of the United States.

Stephanie Fitzgerald has been writing nonfiction for children for more than ten years, and she is the author of more than twenty books. Her specialties include history, wildlife, and popular culture. Stephanie lives in Stamford, Connecticut, with her husband and their daughter.

Page numbers in **boldface** are illustrations.